NAVIGATION RULES

International and Inland

By **United States Coast Guard.**

INTRO VIDEO

https://www.youtube.com/watch?v=8_ixWudmnkc

Contents

All the videos are here. Point your phone code reader at this code and get immediate access to the videos which explain the rules in video format.
SAVE TO THE HOME SCREEN to create an app.

U.S.C.G. Web Site.
(use the QR scanner on your phone available from the app store)

http://www.navcen.uscg.gov/?pageName=navRulesContent

www.TheBoatBookShop.com

Online info at www.navcen.uscg.gov

PART A - GENERAL

Rule 1 - Application (International/Inland)

International

(a) These Rules shall apply to all vessels upon the high seas and in all waters connected therewith navigable by seagoing vessels.

b) Nothing in these Rules shall interfere with the operation of special rules made by an appropriate authority for roadsteads, harbors, rivers, lakes, or inland waterways connected with the high seas and navigable by seagoing vessels. Such special rules shall conform as closely as possible to these Rules

(c) Nothing in these Rules shall interfere with the operation of any special rules made by the Government of any State with respect to additional station or signal lights, shape or whistle signals for ships of war and vessels proceeding under convoy, or with respect to additional station or signal lights or shapes for fishing vessels engaged in fishing as a fleet. These additional stations or signal lights, shapes or whistle signals shall, so far as possible, be such

Inland

(a) These rules apply to all vessels upon the inland waters of the United States, and to vessels of the United States on the Canadian waters of the Great Lakes to the extent that there is no conflict with Canadian law.

(b) (i)These rules constitute special rules made by an appropriate authority within the meaning of Rule 1(b) of the International Regulations. (ii) All vessels complying with the construction and equipment requirements of the International Regulations are considered to be in compliance with these Rules

(c) Nothing in these Rules shall interfere with the operation of any special rules made by the Secretary of the Navy with respect to additional station or signal lights and shapes or whistle signals for ships of war and vessels proceeding under convoy, or by the Secretary with respect to additional station or signal lights and shapes for fishing vessels engaged in fishing as a fleet. These additional station or signal lights and shapes or whistle signals shall, so far as possible, be such that they cannot be mistaken for any light, that they cannot be mistaken for any light, shape, or signal authorized elsewhere under these Rules.1

1Submarines may display, as a distinctive means of identification, an intermittent flashing amber beacon with a sequence of operation of one flash per second for three (3) seconds followed by a three (3) second off-period (32 CFR 707.7). Other special rules made by the Secretary of the Navy with respect to additional station and signal lights are found in Part 706 of Title 32, Code of Federal Regulations (32 CFR 706).

(d) Traffic separation schemes may be adopted by the Organization for the purpose of these Rules.

(e) Whenever the Government concerned shall have determined that a vessel of special construction or purpose cannot comply fully with the provisions of any of these Rules with respect to number, position, range or arc of visibility of lights or shapes, as well as to the disposition and characteristics of sound-signaling appliances, such vessel shall comply with such other provisions in regard to number, position, range or arc of visibility of lights or shapes, as well as to the disposition and characteristics of sound-signalling appliances, as the Government shall

shape or signal authorized elsewhere under these Rules. Notice of such special rules shall be published in the Federal Register and, after the effective date specified in such notice, they shall have effect as if they were a part of these Rules.[1]

[1]Submarines may display, as a distinctive means of identification, an intermittent flashing amber beacon with a sequence of operation of one flash per second for three (3) seconds followed by a three (3) second off-period (32 CFR 707.7). Other special rules made by the Secretary of the Navy with respect to additional station and signal lights are found in Part 706 of Title 32, Code of Federal Regulations (32 CFR 706).

d) Traffic separation schemes may be established for the purposes of these Rules. Vessel traffic service regulations may be in effect in certain areas

(e) Whenever the Secretary determines that a vessel or class of vessels of special construction or purpose cannot comply fully with the provisions of any of these Rules with respect to the number, position, range, or arc of visibility of lights or shapes, as well as to the disposition and characteristics of sound-signalling appliances, the vessel shall comply with such other provisions in regard to the number, position, range, or arc of visibility of lights or shapes, as well as to the disposition and characteristics of have determined to be the closest possible compliance with these Rules in respect to that vessel.

sound-signalling appliances, as the Secretary shall have determined to be the closest possible compliance with these Rules. The Secretary may issue a certificate of alternative compliance for a vessel or class of vessels specifying the closest possible compliance with these Rules. The Secretary of the Navy shall make these determinations and issue certificates of alternative compliance for vessels of the Navy.

f) The Secretary may accept a certificate of alternative compliance issued by a contracting party to the International Regulations if he determines that the alternative compliance standards of the contracting party are substantially the same as those of the United States

Rule 2 - Rule 2 - Responsibility

(a) Nothing in these Rules shall exonerate any vessel, or the owner, master, or crew thereof, from the consequences of any neglect to comply with these Rules or of the neglect of any precaution which may be required by the ordinary practice of seamen, or by the special circumstances of the case.

(b) In construing and complying with these Rules due regard shall be had to all dangers of navigation and collision and to any special circumstances, including the limitations of the vessels involved, which may make a departure from these Rules necessary to avoid immediate danger.

Rule 3 - General Definitions

For the purpose of these Rules and this Chapter, except where the context otherwise requires:

(a) The word "vessel" includes every description of watercraft, including non-displacement craft, WIG craft [Intl], and seaplanes, used or capable of being used as a means of transportation on water.

(b) The term "power-driven vessel" means any vessel propelled by machinery.

(c) The term "sailing vessel" means any vessel under sail provided that propelling machinery, if fitted, is not being used.

(d) The term "vessel engaged in fishing" means any vessel fishing with nets, lines, trawls, or other fishing apparatus which restrict maneuverability, but does not include a vessel fishing with trolling lines or other fishing apparatus which do not restrict maneuverability.

(e) The term "seaplane" includes any aircraft designed to maneuver on the water.

(f) The term "vessel not under command" means a vessel which through some exceptional circumstance is unable to maneuver as required by these Rules and is therefore unable to keep out of the way of another vessel.

(g) The term "vessel restricted in her ability to maneuver" means a vessel which from the nature of her work is restricted in her ability to maneuver as required by these Rules and is therefore unable to keep out of the way of another vessel. The term "vessels restricted in their ability to maneuver" shall include but not be limited to:

   (i) A vessel engaged in laying, servicing, or picking up a navigational mark, submarine cable or pipeline;
   (ii) A vessel engaged in dredging, surveying or underwater operations;
   (iii) A vessel engaged in replenishment or transferring persons,

provisions or cargo while underway;

(iiii) A vessel engaged in the launching or recovery of aircraft;

(iiiii) A vessel engaged in mine clearance operations;

(iiiiii) A vessel engaged in a towing operation such as severely restricts the towing vessel and her tow in their ability to deviate from their course.

(h) The term "vessel constrained by her draft" means a power-driven vessel which because of her draft in relation to the available depth and width of navigable water is severely restricted in her ability to deviate from the course she is following.

(i/h) The word "underway" means that a vessel is not at anchor, or made fast to the shore, or aground.

(j/i) The words "length" and "breadth" of a vessel mean her length overall and greatest breadth.

(k/j) Vessels shall be deemed to be in sight of one another only when one can be observed visually from the other.

(l/k) The term "restricted visibility" means any condition in which visibility is restricted by fog, mist, falling snow, heavy rainstorms, sandstorms or any other similar causes.

(l) "Western Rivers" means the Mississippi River, its tributaries, South Pass, and Southwest Pass, to the navigational demarcation lines dividing the high seas from harbors, rivers and other inland waters of the United States, and the Port Allen-Morgan City Alternate Route, and that part of the Atchafalaya River above its junction with the Port Allen-Morgan City Alternate Route including the Old River and the Red River; [Inld]

(m) The term "Wing-In-Ground (WIG) craft" means a multimodal craft which, in its main operational mode, flies in close proximity to the surface by utilizing surface-effect action. [Intl]

(m1) "Great Lakes" means the Great Lakes and their connecting tributary waters including the Calumet River as far as the Thomas J. O'Brien Lock and

Controlling Waters (between mile 326 and 327), the Chicago River as far as the east side of the Ashland Avenue Bridge (between mile 321 and 322), and the Saint Lawrence River as far east as the lower exit of Saint Lambert Lock; [Inld]

(n) "Secretary" means the Secretary of the department in which the Coast Guard is operating; [Inld]

(o) "Inland Waters" means the navigable waters of the United States shoreward of the navigational demarcation lines dividing the high seas from harbors, rivers and other inland waters of the United States and the waters of the Great Lakes on the United States side of the International Boundary; [Inld]

(p) "Inland Rules" or "Rules" mean the Inland Navigational Rules and the annexes thereto, which govern the conduct of vessels and specify the lights, shapes, and sound signals that apply on inland waters; and [Inld]

(q) "International Regulations" means the International Regulations for Preventing Collisions as Sea, 1972, including annexes currently in force for the United States. [Inld]

PART B - STEERING AND SAILING RULES

Section/Subpart I - Conduct of Vessels in Any Condition of Visibility.

Rule 4 - Application

Rules in this section apply to any condition of visibility.

Rule 5 - Lookout

Every vessel shall at all times maintain a proper look-out by sight and hearing as well as by all available means appropriate in the prevailing circumstances and conditions so as to make a full appraisal of the situation and of the risk of collision.

Rule 6 - Safe Speed

Every vessel shall at all times proceed at a safe speed so that she can take proper and effective action to avoid collision and be stopped within a distance appropriate to the prevailing circumstances and conditions.

In determining a safe speed the following factors shall be among those taken into account:

(a) By all vessels:

(i) The state of visibility;
(ii) The traffic density including concentrations of fishing vessels or any other vessels;
(iii) The manageability of the vessel with special reference to stopping distance and turning ability in the prevailing conditions;
(iiii) At night, the presence of background light such as from shore lights or from back scatter from her own lights;
(iiiii) The state of wind, sea and current, and the proximity of navigational hazards;
(iiiiii) The draft in relation to the available depth of water.

(b) Additionally, by vessels with operational radar:

(i) The characteristics, efficiency and limitations of the radar equipment;
(ii) Any constraints imposed by the radar range scale in use;
(iii) The effect on radar detection of the sea state, weather and other sources of interference;
(iiii) The possibility that small vessels, ice and other floating objects may not be detected by radar at an adequate range;
(iiii) The number, location and movement of vessels detected by radar;
(iii) The more exact assessment of the visibility that may be possible when radar is used to determine the range of vessels or other objects in the vicinity.

Rule 7 - Risk of Collision

(a) Every vessel shall use all available means appropriate to the prevailing circumstances and conditions to determine if risk of collision exists. If there is any doubt such risk shall be deemed to exist.

(b) Proper use shall be made of radar equipment if fitted and operational, including long-range scanning to obtain early warning of risk of collision and radar plotting or equivalent systematic observation of detected objects.

(c) Assumptions shall not be made on the basis of scanty information, especially scanty radar information.

(d) In determining if risk of collision exists the following considerations shall be among those taken into account:

> (i) Such risk shall be deemed to exist if the compass bearing of an approaching vessel does not appreciably change.
> (ii) Such risk may sometimes exist even when an appreciable bearing change is evident, particularly when approaching a very large vessel or a tow or when approaching a vessel at close range.

Rule 8 - Action to Avoid Collision

(a) Any action taken to avoid collision shall be taken in accordance with the Rules of this Part and [Intl] shall, if the circumstances of the case admit, be positive, made in ample time and with due regard to the observance of good seamanship.

(b) Any alteration of course and/or speed to avoid collision shall, if the circumstances of the case admit, be large enough to be readily apparent to another vessel observing visually or by radar; a succession of small alterations of course and/or speed should be avoided.

(c) If there is sufficient sea room, alteration of course alone may be the most effective action to avoid a close-quarters situation provided that it is made in good time, is substantial and does not result in another close-quarters situation.

(d) Action taken to avoid collision with another vessel shall be such as to result in passing at a safe distance. The effectiveness of the action shall be carefully checked until the other vessel is finally past and clear.

(e) If necessary to avoid collision or allow more time to assess the situation, a vessel may slacken her speed or take all way off by stopping or reversing her means of propulsion.

(f) (i) A vessel which, by any of these rules, is required not to impede the passage or safe passage of another vessel shall, when required by the circumstances of the case, take early action to allow sufficient sea room for the safe passage of the other vessel.

(ii) A vessel required not to impede the passage or safe passage of another vessel is not relieved of this obligation if approaching the other vessel so as to involve risk of collision and shall, when taking action, have full regard to the action which may be required by the rules of this part.

(iii) A vessel, the passage of which is not to be impeded remains fully obliged to comply with the rules of this part when the two vessels are approaching one another so as to involve risk of collision.

Rule 9 - Narrow Channels

(a) (i) [Inld] A vessel proceeding along the course of a narrow channel or fairway shall keep as near to the outer limit of the channel or fairway which lies on her starboard side as is safe and practicable.

(ii) Notwithstanding paragraph (a)(i) and Rule 14(a), a power-driven vessel operating in narrow channels or fairways on the Great Lakes, Western Rivers, or waters specified by the Secretary, and proceeding downbound with a following current shall have the right-of-way over an upbound vessel, shall propose the manner and place of passage, and shall initiate the maneuvering signals prescribed by Rule 34(a)(i), as appropriate. The vessel proceeding upbound against the current shall hold as necessary to permit safe passing. [Inld]

(b) A vessel of less than 20 meters in length or a sailing vessel shall not impede the passage of a vessel which can safely navigate only within a narrow channel or fairway.

(c) A vessel engaged in fishing shall not impede the passage of any other vessel navigating within a narrow channel or fairway.

(d) A vessel shall not cross a narrow passage or fairway if such crossing impedes the passage of a vessel which can safely navigate only within such channel or fairway. The latter vessel may use the sound signal prescribed in Rule 34(d) if in doubt as to the intention of the crossing vessel.

(e)

International

(i) In a narrow channel or fairway when overtaking can take place only if the vessel to be overtaken has to take action to permit safe passing, the vessel intending to overtake shall indicate her intention by sounding the appropriate signal prescribed in Rule 34(c)(i). The vessel to be overtaken shall, if in agreement, sound the appropriate signal prescribed in Rule 34(c)(ii) and take steps to permit safe passing. If in doubt she may sound the signals prescribed in Rule 34(d).

Inland

(i) In a narrow channel or fairway when overtaking, the power-driven vessel intending to overtake another power-driven vessel shall indicate her intention by sounding the appropriate signal prescribed in Rule 34(c) and take steps to permit safe passing. The power-driven vessel being overtaken, if in agreement, shall sound the same signal and may, if specifically agreed to take steps to permit safe passing. If in doubt, she shall sound the danger signal prescribed in Rule 34(d).

(ii) This rule does not relieve the overtaking vessel of her obligation under Rule 13.

(f) A vessel nearing a bend or an area of a narrow channel or fairway where other vessels may be obscured by an intervening obstruction shall navigate with particular alertness and caution and shall sound the appropriate signal prescribed in Rule 34(e).

(g) Any vessel shall, if the circumstances of the case admit, avoid anchoring in a narrow channel.

Rule 10 - Traffic Separation Schemes/Vessel Traffic Services

(a) This Rule applies to traffic separation schemes adopted by the Organization [Intl] and does not relieve any vessel of her obligation under any other rule.

(b) A vessel using a traffic separation scheme shall:

(i) Proceed in the appropriate traffic lane in the general direction of traffic flow for that lane.
(ii) So far as is practicable keep clear of a traffic separation line or separation zone.
(iii) Normally join or leave a traffic lane at the termination of the lane, but when joining or leaving from either side shall do so at as small an angle to the general direction of traffic flow as practicable.

(c) A vessel, shall so far as practicable, avoid crossing traffic lanes but if obliged to do so shall cross on a heading as nearly as practicable at right angles to the general direction of traffic flow.

(d) (i) A vessel shall not use an inshore traffic zone when she can safely use the appropriate traffic lane within the adjacent traffic separation scheme. However, vessels of less than 20 meters in length, sailing vessels and vessels engaged in fishing may use the inshore traffic zone.

(ii) Notwithstanding subparagraph (d)(i), a vessel may use an inshore traffic zone when en route to or from a port, offshore installation or structure, pilot station or any other place situated within the inshore traffic zone, or to avoid immediate danger.

(e) A vessel, other than a crossing vessel or a vessel joining or leaving a lane shall not normally enter a separation zone or cross a separation line except:

(i) in cases of emergency to avoid immediate danger;
(ii) to engage in fishing within a separation zone.

(f) A vessel navigating in areas near the terminations of traffic separation schemes shall do so with particular caution.

(g) A vessel shall so far as practicable avoid anchoring in a traffic separation scheme or in areas near its terminations.

(h) A vessel not using a traffic separating scheme shall avoid it by as wide a margin as is practicable.

(i) A vessel engaged in fishing shall not impede the passage of any vessel following a traffic lane.

(j) A vessel of less than 20 meters in length or a sailing vessel shall not impede the safe passage of a power-driven vessel following a traffic lane.

(k) A vessel restricted in her ability to maneuver when engaged in an operation for the maintenance of safety of navigation in a traffic separation scheme is exempted from complying with this Rule to the extent necessary to carry out the operation.

(l) A vessel restricted in her ability to maneuver when engaged in an operation for the laying, servicing or picking up of a submarine cable, within a traffic separation scheme, is exempted from complying with this Rule to the extent necessary to carry out the operation.

Section/Subpart II - Conduct of Vessels in Sight of One Another

Rule 11 - Application

Rules in this section apply to vessels in sight of one another.

Rule 12 - Sailing Vessels

(a) When two sailing vessels are approaching one another, so as to involve risk of collision, one of them shall keep out of the way of the other as follows:

(i) when each has the wind on a different side, the vessel which has the wind on the port side shall keep out of the way of the other;
(ii) when both have the wind on the same side, the vessel which is to windward shall keep out of the way of the vessel which is to leeward;

(iii) if a vessel with the wind on the port side sees a vessel to windward and cannot determine with certainty whether the other vessel has the wind on the port or on the starboard side, she shall keep out of the way of the other.

(b) For the purposes of this Rule the windward side shall be deemed to be the side opposite that on which the mainsail is carried or, in the case of a square-rigged vessel, the side opposite to that on which the largest fore-and-aft sail is carried.

Rule 13 - Overtaking

(a) Notwithstanding anything contained in the Rules [of Part B, Sections I and II / 4 through 18], any vessel overtaking any other shall keep out of the way of the vessel being overtaken.

(b) A vessel shall be deemed to be overtaking when coming up with a another vessel from a direction more than 22.5 degrees abaft her beam, that is, in such a position with reference to the vessel she is overtaking, that at night she would be able to see only the sternlight of that vessel but neither of her sidelights.

(c) When a vessel is in any doubt as to whether she is overtaking another, she shall assume that this is the case and act accordingly.

(d) Any subsequent alteration of the bearing between the two vessels shall not make the overtaking vessel a crossing vessel within the meaning of these Rules or relieve her of the duty of keeping clear of the overtaken vessel until she is finally past and clear.

Rule 14 - Head-on Situation

(a) Unless otherwise agreed [Inld] When two power-driven vessels are meeting on reciprocal or nearly reciprocal courses so as to involve risk of collision each shall alter her course to starboard so that each shall pass on the port side of the other.

(b) Such a situation shall be deemed to exist when a vessel sees the other ahead or nearly ahead and by night she could see the masthead lights of the other in a line or nearly in a line and/ [Intl] or both sidelights and by day she observes the corresponding aspect of the other vessel.

(c) When a vessel is in any doubt as to whether such a situation exists she shall assume that it does exist and act accordingly.

(d) Notwithstanding paragraph (a) of this Rule, a power-driven vessel operating on the Great Lakes, Western Rivers, or waters specified by the Secretary, and proceeding downbound with a following current shall have the right-of-way over an upbound vessel, shall propose the manner of passage, and shall initiate the maneuvering signals prescribed by Rule 34(a)(i), as appropriate. [Inld]

Rule 15 - Crossing Situation

When two power-driven vessels are crossing so as to involve risk of collision, the vessel which has the other on her own starboard side shall keep out of the way and shall, if the circumstances of the case admit, avoid crossing ahead of the other vessel.

(b) Notwithstanding paragraph (a), on the Great Lakes, Western Rivers, or water specified by the Secretary, a power-driven vessel crossing a river shall keep out of the way of a power-driven vessel ascending or descending the river. [Inld]

Rule 16 - Action by Give-way Vessel

Every vessel which is directed to keep out of the way of another vessel shall, so far as possible, take early and substantial action to keep well clear.

Rule 17- Action by Stand-on Vessel

18

(a) (i) Where one of two vessels is to keep out of the way, the other shall keep her course and speed.

(ii) The latter vessel may however take action to avoid collision by her maneuver alone, as soon as it becomes apparent to her that the vessel required to keep out of the way is not taking appropriate action in compliance with these Rules.
(b) When, from any cause, the vessel required to keep her course and speed finds herself so close that collision cannot be avoided by the action of the give-way vessel alone, she shall take such action as will best aid to avoid collision.

(c) A power-driven vessel which takes action in a crossing situation in accordance with subparagraph (a)(ii) of this Rule to avoid collision with another power-driven vessel shall, if the circumstances of the case admit, not alter course to port for a vessel on her own port side.

(d) This Rule does not relieve the give-way vessel of her obligation to keep out of the way.

Rule 18 - Responsibilities Between Vessels

Except where Rules 9, 10, and 13 otherwise require:

(a) A power-driven vessel underway shall keep out of the way of:
(i) a vessel not under command;
(ii) a vessel restricted in her ability to maneuver;
(iii) a vessel engaged in fishing;
(iiii) a sailing vessel.
(b) A sailing vessel underway shall keep out of the way of:

(i) a vessel not under command;
(ii) a vessel restricted in her ability to maneuver;
(iii) a vessel engaged in fishing.
(c) A vessel engaged in fishing when underway shall, so far as possible, keep

out of the way of:

> (i) a vessel not under command;
>
> (ii) a vessel restricted in her ability to maneuver.

(d) (i) Any vessel other than a vessel not under command or a vessel restricted in her ability to maneuver shall, if the circumstances of the case admit, avoid impeding the safe passage of a vessel constrained by her draft, exhibiting the signals in Rule 28.

> (ii) A vessel constrained by her draft shall navigate with particular caution having full regard to her special condition. [Intl]

(e/d) A seaplane on the water shall, in general, keep well clear of all vessels and avoid impeding their navigation. In circumstances, however, where risk of collision exists, she shall comply with the Rules of this Part.

(f) (i) A WIG craft shall, when taking off, landing and in flight near the surface, keep well clear of all other vessels and avoid impeding their navigation;

(ii) a WIG craft operating on the water surface shall comply with the Rules of this Part as a power-driven vessel.

Section/Subpart III - Conduct of Vessels in Restricted Visibility

Rule 19 - Conduct of Vessels in Restricted Visibility

(a) This Rule applies to vessels not in sight of one another when navigating in or near an area of restricted visibility.

(b) Every vessel shall proceed at a safe speed adapted to the prevailing circumstances and conditions of restricted visibility. A power-driven vessel shall have her engines ready for immediate maneuver.

(c) Every vessel shall have due regard to the prevailing circumstances and conditions of restricted visibility when complying with the Rules [of Section I of this Part / 4 through 10].

(d) A vessel which detects by radar alone the presence of another vessel shall determine if a close-quarters situation is developing and/ [Intl] or risk of collision exists. If so, she shall take avoiding action in ample time, provided that when such action consists of an alteration in course, so far as possible the following shall be avoided:

(i) An alteration of course to port for a vessel forward of the beam, other than for a vessel being overtaken;

(ii) An alteration of course toward a vessel abeam or abaft the beam.

(e) Except where it has been determined that a risk of collision does not exist, every vessel which hears apparently forward of her beam the fog signal of another vessel, or which cannot avoid a close-quarters situation with another vessel forward of her beam, shall reduce her speed to be the minimum at which she can be kept on her course. She shall if necessary take all her way off and in any event navigate with extreme caution until danger of collision is over.

PART C - LIGHTS AND SHAPES

Rule 20 - Application

(a) Rules in this part shall be complied with in all weathers.

(b) The Rules concerning lights shall be complied with from sunset to sunrise, and during such times no other lights shall be exhibited, except such lights which cannot be mistaken for the lights specified in these Rules or do not impair their visibility or distinctive character, or interfere with the keeping of a proper look-out.

(c) The lights prescribed by these Rules shall, if carried, also be exhibited from sunrise to sunset in restricted visibility and may be exhibited in all other circumstances when it is deemed necessary.

(d) The Rules concerning shapes shall be complied with by day.

(e) The lights and shapes specified in these Rules shall comply with the provisions of Annex I [to these Regulations/of these Rules].

Rule 21 - Definitions

(a) "Masthead light" means a white light placed over the fore and aft centerline of the vessel showing an unbroken light over an arc of the horizon of 225 degrees and so fixed as to show the light from right ahead to 22.5 degrees abaft the beam on either side of the vessel, except that on a vessel of less than 12 meters in length the masthead light shall be placed as nearly as practicable to the fore and aft centerline of the vessel. [Inld]

(b) "Sidelights" means a green light on the starboard side and a red light on the port side each showing an unbroken light over an arc of the horizon of 112.5 degrees and so fixed as to show the light from right ahead to 22.5 degrees abaft the beam on its respective side. In a vessel of less than 20 meters in length the sidelights may be combined in one lantern carried on the fore and aft centerline of the vessel, except that on a vessel of less than 12 meters in length the sidelights when combined in one lantern shall be placed as nearly as practicable to the fore and aft centerline of the vessel. [Inld]

(c) "Sternlight" means a white light placed as nearly as practicable at the stern showing an unbroken light over an arc of the horizon of 135 degrees and so fixed as to show the light 67.5 degrees from right aft on each side of the vessel.

(d) "Towing light" means a yellow light having the same characteristics as the "sternlight" defined in paragraph (c) of this Rule.

(e) "All-round light" means a light showing an unbroken light over an arc of the horizon of 360 degrees.

(f) "Flashing light" means a light flashing at regular intervals at a frequency of 120 flashes or more per minute.

(g) "Special flashing light" means a yellow light flashing at regular intervals at a frequency of 50 to 70 flashes per minute, placed as far forward and as nearly as practicable on the fore and aft centerline of the tow and showing an unbroken light over an arc of the horizon of not less than 180 degrees nor more than 225 degrees and so fixed as to show the light from right ahead to abeam and no more than 22.5 degrees abaft the beam on either side of the vessel. [Inld]

A Graphical Representation of Rule 21 & 22 Navigation Lights Arcs and Ranges of Visibility

Masthead Light;Starbord Sidelight; Port Sidelight; Stern Light; Towing Light; Special Flashing Light

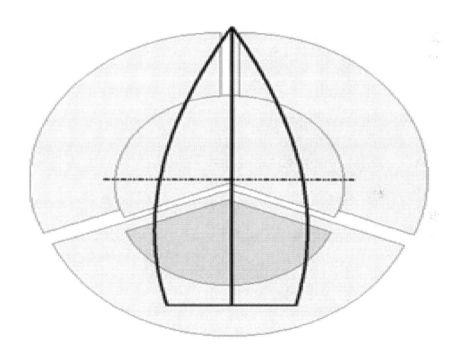

Rule 22 - Visibility of Lights

The lights prescribed in these Rules shall have an intensity as specified in Section 8 [Intl] of Annex I to these [Regulations / Rules] so as to be visible at the following minimum ranges:

(a) In vessels of 50 meters or more in length:

(i) a masthead light, 6 miles;
(ii) a sidelight, 3 miles;
(iii) a towing light, 3 miles;
(iiii) a white red, green or yellow all-round light, 3 miles.
(iiiii) a special flashing light, 2 miles. [Inld]

(b) In vessels of 12 meters or more in length but less than 50 meters in length;

(i) a masthead light, 5 miles; except that where the length of the vessel is less than 20 meters, 3 miles;
(ii) a sidelight, 2 miles;
(iii) a sternlight, 2 miles;
(iii) a towing light, 2 miles;
(iiii) a white, red, green or yellow all-round light, 2 miles.
(iiiii) a special flashing light, 2 miles. [Inld]

(c) In vessels of less than 12 meters in length:

(i) a masthead light, 2 miles;
(ii) a sidelight, 1 miles;
(iii) a towing light, 2 miles;
(iiii) a white red, green or yellow all-round light, 2 miles.
(iiiii) a special flashing light, 2 miles. [Inld]

(d) In inconspicuous, partly submerged vessels or objects being towed;

(i) a white all-round light; 3 miles.

Rule 23 - Power-driven Vessels Underway

(a) A power-driven vessel underway shall exhibit (picture):
(i) a masthead light forward;
(ii) a second masthead light abaft of and higher than the forward one; except that a vessel of less than 50 meters in length shall not be obliged to exhibit such a light but may do so;
(iii) sidelights: and
(iiii) a sternlight.

24

(b) An air-cushion vessel when operating in nondisplacement mode shall, in addition to the lights prescribed in paragraph (a) of this Rule, exhibit an all-round flashing yellow light, where it can best be seen. [Inld]

(c) A WIG craft only when taking off, landing and in flight near the surface shall, in addition to the lights prescribed in paragraph (a) of this Rule, exhibit a high intensity all-round flashing red light. [Intl]

(c/d) (i) A power-driven vessel of less than 12 meters in length may in lieu of the lights prescribed in paragraph (a) of this Rule exhibit an all-round white light and sidelights.
(ii) a power-driven vessel of less than 7 meters in length whose maximum speed does not exceed 7 knots may in lieu of the lights prescribed in paragraph (a) of this Rule exhibit an all-round white light and shall, if practicable, also exhibit sidelights. [Intl]
(iii) the masthead light or all-round white light on a power-driven vessel of less than 12 meters in length may be displaced from the fore and aft centerline of the vessel if centerline fitting is not practicable, provided the sidelights are combined in one lantern which shall be carried on the fore and aft centerline of the vessel or located as nearly as practicable in the same fore and aft line as the masthead light or the all-round white light. [Intl]
(d) A power-driven vessel when operating on the Great Lakes may carry an all-round white light in lieu of the second masthead light and sternlight prescribed in paragraph (a) of this Rule. The light shall be carried in the position of the second masthead light and be visible at the same minimum range. [Inld]

Rule 24 - Towing and Pushing

(a) A power-driven vessel when towing astern [Inld] shall exhibit:

(i) Instead of the light prescribed in Rule 23(a)(i) or 23(a)(ii), two masthead lights in a vertical line. When the length of the tow, measuring from the stern of the towing vessel to the after end of the tow exceeds 200 meters, three such lights in a vertical line;

(ii) sidelights;

(iii) a sternlight;

(iiii) a towing light in a vertical line above the sternlight; and

(iiiii) when the length of the tow exceeds 200 meters, a diamond shape where it can best be seen.

(b) When a pushing vessel and a vessel being pushed ahead are rigidly connected in a composite unit they shall be regarded as a power-driven vessel and exhibit the lights prescribed in Rule 23. (pictures of a unit over 50m/ unit less than 50m)

(c) A power-driven vessel when pushing ahead or towing alongside, except [in the case of a composite unit / as required by paragraphs (b) and (i) of this Rule], shall exhibit:

(i) instead of the light prescribed in Rule 23(a)(i) or 23(a)(ii), two masthead lights in a vertical line;

(ii) sidelights; and

(iii) [a sternlight / two towing lights in a vertical line]

(d) A power-driven vessel to which paragraph (a) or (c) of this Rule apply shall also comply with rule 23(a)(i) [Inld] and 23(a)(ii). (picture of vessel with tow 200m or less AND less than 50m in length / 50m or more in length)

(e) A vessel or object being towed, other than those mentioned in paragraph (g) of this Rule, shall exhibit:

(i) sidelights;

(ii) a sternlight;

(iii) when the length of the tow exceeds 200 meters, a diamond shape where it can best be seen.

(f) Provided that any number of vessels being towed alongside or pushed in a group shall be lighted as one vessel, except as provided in paragraph (iii) [Inld] (pictures of International and Inland configurations)

(i) a vessel being pushed ahead, not being part of a composite unit, shall exhibit at the forward end, sidelights, and a special flashing light [Inld];

(ii) a vessel being towed alongside shall exhibit a sternlight and at the forward end, sidelights, and a special flashing light [Inld];

(iii) when vessels are towed alongside on both sides of the towing vessels a sternlight shall be exhibited on the stern of the outboard vessel on each side of the towing vessel, and a single set of sidelights as far forward an as far outboard as is practicable, and a single special flashing light [Inld];

(g) An inconspicuous, partly submerged vessel or object, or combination of such vessels or objects being towed, [Intl] shall exhibit:

International

(i) if it is less than 25 meters in breadth, one all-round white light at or near the forward end and one at or near the after end except that dracones need not exhibit a light at or near the forward end.
(ii) if it is 25 meters or more in breadth, two or more additional all-round white lights at or near the extremities of its breadth;

Inland

(i) if it is less than 25 meters in breadth, one all-round white light at or near each end.
(ii) if it is 25 meters or more in breadth, four all-round white lights to mark its length and breadth;

(iii) if it exceeds 100 meters in length, additional all-round white lights between the lights prescribed in subparagraphs (i) and (ii) so that the distance between the lights shall not exceed 100 meters. Provided, that any vessels or objects being towed alongside each other shall be lighted as one vessel or object [Inld];
(iiii) a diamond shape at or near the aftermost extremity of the last vessel or object being towed and if the length of the tow exceeds 200 meters an additional diamond shape where it can best be seen and located as far forward as is practicable. [Intl]
(iiiii) the towing vessel may direct a searchlight in the direction of the tow to indicate its presence to an approaching vessel. [Inld]
(h) When from any sufficient cause it is impracticable for a vessel or object being towed to exhibit the lights or shapes [Intl] prescribed in paragraph (e) or (g) of this Rule, all possible measures shall be taken to light the vessel or object being towed or at least indicate the presence of [such / unlighted] vessel

or object.

(i) Notwithstanding paragraph (c), on the Western Rivers (except below the Huey P. Long Bridge on the Mississippi River) and on waters specified by the Secretary, a power-driven vessel when pushing ahead or towing alongside, except as paragraph (b) applies, shall exhibit: [Inld]

    (i) sidelights; and [Inld]
    (ii) two towing lights in a vertical line. [Inld]

(i/j) Where from any sufficient cause it is impracticable for a vessel not normally engaged in towing operations to display the lights prescribed in paragraph (a), (c) or (i) [Inld] of this Rule, such vessel shall not be required to exhibit those lights when engaged in towing another vessel in distress or otherwise in need of assistance. All possible measures shall be taken to indicate the nature of the relationship between the towing vessel and the vessel being towed as authorized by Rule 36, in particular by illuminating the [towline/tow].

Rule 25 - Sailing Vessels Underway and Vessels Under Oars

(a) A sailing vessel underway shall exhibit:
(i) sidelights;
(ii) a sternlight.
(b) In a sailing vessel of less than 20 meters in length the lights prescribed in paragraph (a) of this Rule may be combined in one lantern carried at or near the top of the mast where it can best be seen.

(c) A sailing vessel underway may, in addition to the lights prescribed in paragraph (a) of this Rule, exhibit at or near the top of the mast, where they can best be seen,two all-round lights in a vertical line, the upper being red and the lower Green, but these lights shall not be exhibited in conjunction with the combined lantern permitted by paragraph (b) of this Rule.

(d) (i) A sailing vessel of less than 7 meters in length shall, if practicable, exhibit the lights prescribed in paragraph (a) or (b) of this Rule, but if she does not, she shall have ready at hand an electric torch or lighted lantern showing a white light which shall be exhibited in sufficient time to prevent collision.

(ii) A vessel under oars may exhibit the lights prescribed in this rule for sailing vessels, but if she does not, she shall have ready at hand an electric torch or lighted lantern showing a white light which shall be exhibited in sufficient time to prevent collision.

(e) A vessel proceeding under sail when also being propelled by machinery shall exhibit forward where it can best be seen a conical shape, apex downwards. A vessel of less than 12 meters in length is not required to exhibit this shape, but may do so. [Inld]

Rule 26 - Fishing Vessels

(a) A vessel engaged in fishing, whether underway or at anchor, shall exhibit only the lights and shapes prescribed in this Rule.

(b) A vessel when engaged in trawling, by which is meant the dragging through the water of a dredge net or other apparatus used as a fishing appliance, shall exhibit:

(i) two all-round lights in a vertical line, the upper being green and the lower white, or a shape consisting of two cones with their apexes together in a vertical line one above the other;

(ii) a masthead light abaft of and higher than the all-round green light; a vessel of less than 50 meters in length shall not be obliged to exhibit such a light but may do so;

(iii) when making way through the water, in addition to the lights prescribed in this paragraph, sidelights and a sternlight.

(c) A vessel engaged in fishing, other than trawling, shall exhibit:

(i) two all-round lights in a vertical line, the upper being red and the lower white, or a shape consisting of two cones with their apexes together in a vertical line one above the other;

(ii) when there is outlying gear extending more than 150 meters horizontally from the vessel, an all-round white light or a cone apex upwards in the direction of the gear.

(iii) when making way through the water, in addition to the lights prescribed in this paragraph, sidelights and a sternlight.

(d) The additional signals described in Annex II to these Rules apply to a vessel engaged in fishing in close proximity to other vessels engaged in fishing.

(e) A vessel when not engaged in fishing shall not exhibit the lights or shapes prescribed in this Rule, but only those prescribed for a vessel of her length.

Rule 27 - Vessels Not Under Command or Restricted in Their Ability to Maneuver

(a) A vessel not under command shall exhibit:
(i) two all-round red lights in a vertical line where they can best be seen;
(ii) two balls or similar shapes in a vertical line where they can best be seen;
(iii) when making way through the water, in addition to the lights prescribed in this paragraph, sidelights and a sternlight.
(b) A vessel restricted in her ability to maneuver, except a vessel engaged in mineclearance operations, shall exhibit:
(i) three all-round lights in a vertical line where they can best be seen. The highest and lowest of these lights shall be red and the middle light shall be white;
(ii) three shapes in a vertical line where they can best be seen. The highest and lowest of these shapes shall be balls and the middle one a diamond.
(iii) when making way through the water, [a masthead light or lights/ masthead lights], sidelights and a sternlight in addition to the lights prescribed in subparagraph (b)(i);
(iiii) when at anchor, in addition to the lights or shapes prescribed in subparagraphs (b)(i) and (b) (ii), the light, lights, or shapes prescribed in Rule 30.
(c) A power-driven vessel engaged in a towing operation such as severely restricts the towing vessel and her tow in their ability to deviate from their course shall, in addition to the lights or shapes prescribed in [Rule 24(a) / subparagraph (b)(i) and (ii) of this Rule], exhibit the lights or shape prescribed in [subparagraph (b)(i) and (ii) of this Rule / Rule 24].

(d) A vessel engaged in dredging or underwater operations, when restricted in her ability to maneuver, shall exhibit the lights and shapes prescribed in subparagraphs(b)(i),(ii) and (iii) of this Rule and shall in addition when an obstruction exists, exhibit:

(i) two all-round red lights or two balls in a vertical line to indicate the side on which the obstruction exists;

(ii) two all-round green lights or two diamonds in a vertical line to indicate the side on which another vessel may pass;

(iii) when at anchor, the lights or shapes prescribed in this paragraph instead of the lights or shapes prescribed in Rule 30, for anchored vessels. [Inld]

(e) Whenever the size of a vessel engaged in diving operations makes it impracticable to exhibit all lights and shapes prescribed in paragraph (d) of this Rule, the following shall be exhibited:

(i) Three all-round lights in a vertical line where they can best be seen. The highest and lowest of these lights shall be red and the middle light shall be white;

(ii) a rigid replica of the International Code flag "A" not less than 1 meter in height. Measures shall be taken to ensure its all-round visibility.

(f) A vessel engaged in mineclearance operations shall, in addition to the lights prescribed for a power-driven vessel in Rule 23 or to the lights or shape prescribed for a vessel at anchor in Rule 30 as appropriate, exhibit three all-round green lights or three balls. One of these lights or shapes shall be exhibited near the foremast head and one at each end of the fore yard. These lights or shapes indicate that it is dangerous for another vessel to approach within 1000 meters of the mineclearance vessel.

(g) Vessels of less than 12 meters in length, except those engaged in diving operations, shall not be required to exhibit the lights prescribed in this Rule.

(h) The signals prescribed in this Rule are not signals of vessels in distress and requiring assistance. Such signals are contained in Annex IV to these [Regulations / Rules].

Rule 28 - Vessels Constrained by Their Draft

(INTERNATIONAL ONLY)
A vessel constrained by her draft may, in addition to the lights prescribed for power-driven vessels in Rule 23, exhibit where they can best be seen three all-round red lights in a vertical line, or a cylinder.

Rule 29 - Pilot Vessels

(a) A vessel engaged on pilotage duty shall exhibit:
(i) at or near the masthead, two all-round lights in a vertical line, the upper being white and the lower red;
(ii) when underway, in addition, sidelights and a sternlight;
(iii) when at anchor, in addition to the lights prescribed in subparagraph (i), the light, lights, or shape prescribed in Rule 30 for [vessels at anchor / anchored vessels].
(b) A pilot vessel when not engaged on pilotage duty shall exhibit the lights or shapes prescribed for a similar vessel of her length.

Rule 30 - Anchored Vessels and Vessels Aground

(a) A vessel at anchor shall exhibit where it can best be seen:
(i) in the fore part, an all-round white light or one ball;
(ii) at or near the stern and at a lower level than the light prescribed in subparagraph (i), an all-round white light.
(b) A vessel of less than 50 meters in length may exhibit an all-round white light where it can best be seen instead of the lights prescribed in paragraph (a) of this Rule.

(c) A vessel at anchor may, and a vessel of 100 meters and more in length shall, also use the available working or equivalent lights to illuminate her decks.

(d) A vessel aground shall exhibit the lights prescribed in paragraph (a) or (b) of this Rule and in addition, if practicable, [Inld] where they can best be seen;

(i) two all-round red lights in a vertical line;
(ii) three balls in a vertical line.

(e) A vessel of less than 7 meters in length, when at anchor not in or near a narrow channel, fairway or where other vessels normally navigate, shall not be required to exhibit the shape prescribed in paragraphs (a) and (b) of this Rule.

(f) A vessel of less than 12 meters in length, when aground, shall not be required to exhibit the lights or shapes prescribed in subparagraphs (d)(i) and (ii) of this Rule.

(g) A vessel of less than 20 meters in length, when at anchor in a special anchorage area designated by the Secretary, shall not be required to exhibit the anchor lights and shapes required by this Rule. [Inld]

Rule 31 - Seaplanes

Where it is impracticable for a seaplane or a WIG craft [Intl] to exhibit lights or shapes of the characteristics or in the positions prescribed in the Rules of this Part she shall exhibit lights and shapes as closely similar in characteristics and position as is possible.

PART D - SOUND AND LIGHT SIGNALS

Rule 32 - Definitions

(a) The word "whistle" means any sound signalling appliance capable of producing the prescribed blasts and which complies with the specifications in Annex III to these [Regulations / Rules].

(b) The term "short blast" means a blast of about one second's duration.

(c) The term "prolonged blast" means a blast of from four to six seconds' duration.

Rule 33 - Equipment for Sound Signals

(a) A vessel of 12 meters or more in length shall be provided with a whistle and a bell [INLD], a vessel of 20 meters or more in length shall be provided with a bell in addition to a whistle [Intl], and a vessel of 100 meters or more in length shall, in addition be provided with a gong, the tone and sound of which cannot be confused with that of the bell. The whistle, bell and gong shall comply with the specifications in Annex III to these Regulations. The bell or gong or both may be replaced by other equipment having the same respective sound characteristics, provided that manual sounding of the prescribed signals shall always be possible.

(b) A vessel of less than 12 meters in length shall not be obliged to carry the sound signaling appliances prescribed in paragraph (a) of this Rule but if she does not, she shall be provided with some other means of making an efficient signal.

Rule 34 - Maneuvering and Warning Signals

INTERNATIONAL

(a) When vessels are in sight of one another, a power-driven vessel underway, when maneuvering as authorized or required by these Rules, shall indicate that maneuver by the following signals on her whistle:

    (i) one short blast to mean "I am altering my course to starboard";

INLAND

a) When power-driven vessels are in sight of one another and meeting or crossing at a distance within half a mile of each other, each vessel underway, when maneuvering as authorized or required by these Rules:

    (i) shall indicate that maneuver by the following signals on her whistle:

- one short blast to mean "I intend to

34

(ii) two short blasts to mean "I am altering my course to port";
(iii) three short blasts to mean "I am operating astern propulsion

(b) Any vessel may supplement the whistle signals prescribed in paragraph (a) of this Rule by light signals, repeated as appropriate, while the maneuver is being carried out:

(i) these signals shall have the following significance:

- one flash to mean "I am altering my course to starboard";

two flashes to mean "I am altering my course to port";

- three flashes to mean "I am operating astern propulsion".

(ii) the duration of each flash

leave you on my port side";

- two short blasts to mean "I intend to leave you on my starboard side";

three short blasts to mean "I am operating astern propulsion".

(ii) upon hearing the one or two blast signal of the other shall, if in agreement, sound the same whistle signal and take the steps necessary to effect a safe passing. If, however, from any cause, the vessel doubts the safety of the proposed maneuver, she shall sound the danger signal specified in paragraph (d) of this Rule and each vessel shall take appropriate precautionary action until a safe passing agreement is made.

(b) Any vessel may supplement the whistle signals prescribed in paragraph (a) of this Rule by light signals:

(i) these signals shall have the following significance:

- one flash to mean "I intend to leave you on my port side";

two flashes to mean "I intend to leave you on my starboard side";

- three flashes to mean "I am operating astern propulsion".

shall be about one second, the interval between flashes shall be about one second, and the interval between successive signals shall not be less than ten seconds.

(iii) the light used for this signal shall, if fitted, be an all-round white light, visible at a minimum range of 5 miles, and shall comply with the provisions of Annex I to these Regulations.

c) When in sight of one another in a narrow channel or fairway:

(i) a vessel intending to overtake another shall in compliance with Rule 9 (e)(i) indicate her intention by the following signals on her whistle:

- two prolonged blasts followed by one short blast to mean "I intend to overtake you on your starboard side"

two prolonged blasts followed by two short blasts to mean "I intend to overtake you on your port side"

(ii) the vessel about to be overtaken when acting in accordance with 9(e)(i) shall indicate her agreement by the following signal on her whistle:

- one prolonged, one short, one prolonged and one short blast, in that order.

(ii) the duration of each flash shall be about one second;

(iii) the light used for this signal shall, if fitted, be an all-round white or yellow light, visible at a minimum range of 2 miles, synchronized with the whistle, and shall comply with the provisions of Annex I to these Rules.

c) When in sight of one another:

(i) a power-driven vessel intending to overtake another power-driven vessel shall indicate her intention by the following signals on her whistle:

- one short blast to mean "I intend to overtake you on your starboard side"

two short blasts to mean "I intend to overtake you on your port side".

(ii) the power-driven vessel about to be overtaken shall, if in agreement, sound a similar signal. If in doubt she shall sound the danger signal prescribed in paragraph (d).

36

(d) When vessels in sight of one another are approaching each other and from any cause either vessel fails to understand the intentions or actions of the other, or is in doubt whether sufficient action is being taken by the other to avoid collision, the vessel in doubt shall immediately indicate such doubt by giving at least five short and rapid blasts on the whistle. [Such / This] signal may be supplemented by at least five short and rapid flashes.

(e) A vessel nearing a bend or an area of a channel or fairway where other vessels may be obscured by an intervening obstruction shall sound one prolonged blast. Such signal shall be answered with a prolonged blast by any approaching vessel that may be within hearing around the bend or behind the intervening obstruction.

(f) If whistles are fitted on a vessel at a distance apart of more than 100 meters, one whistle only shall be used for giving maneuvering and warning signals.

(g) When a power-driven vessel is leaving a dock or berth, she shall sound one prolonged blast. [Inld]

(h) A vessel that reaches agreement with another vessel in a head-on, crossing, or overtaking situation, as for example, by using the radiotelephone as prescribed by the Vessel Bridge-to-Bridge Radiotelephone Act (85 Stat. 164; 33 U.S.C. 1201 et seq.), is not obliged to sound the whistle signals prescribed by this Rule, but may do so. If agreement is not reached, then whistle signals shall be exchanged in a timely manner and shall prevail. [Inld]

Rule 35 - Sound Signals in Restricted Visibility

In or near an area of restricted visibility, whether by day or night the signals prescribed in this Rule shall be used as follows:

(a) A power-driven vessel making way through the water shall sound at intervals of not more than 2 minutes one prolonged blast.

(b) A power-driven vessel underway but stopped and making no way through the water shall sound at intervals of no more than 2 minutes two prolonged blasts in succession with an interval of about 2 seconds between them.

(c) A vessel not under command, a vessel restricted in her ability to maneuver whether underway or at anchor [Inld], a vessel constrained by her draft [Intl], a sailing vessel, a vessel engaged in fishing whether underway or at anchor [Inld] and a vessel engaged in towing or pushing another vessel shall, instead of the signals prescribed in paragraph (a) or (b) of this Rule, sound at intervals of not more than 2 minutes three blasts in succession, namely one prolonged followed by two short blasts.

(d) A vessel engaged in fishing, when at anchor, and a vessel restricted in her ability to maneuver when carrying out her work at anchor, shall instead of the signals prescribed in paragraph (g) of this Rule sound the signal prescribed in paragraph (c) of this Rule. [Intl]

(e/d) A vessel towed or if more than one vessel is towed the last vessel of the tow, if manned, shall at intervals of not more than 2 minutes sound four blasts in succession, namely one prolonged followed by three short blasts. When practicable, this signal shall be made immediately after the signal made by the towing vessel.

(f/e) When a pushing vessel and a vessel being pushed ahead are rigidly connected in a composite unit they shall be regarded as a power-driven vessel and shall give the signals prescribed in paragraphs (a) or (b) of this Rule.

(g/f) A vessel at anchor shall at intervals of not more than 1 minute ring the bell rapidly for about 5 seconds. In a vessel 100 meters or more in length the bell shall be sounded in the forepart of the vessel and immediately after the ringing of the bell the gong shall be sounded rapidly for about 5 seconds in the after part of the vessel. A vessel at anchor may in addition sound three blasts in succession, namely one short, one long and one short blast, to give warning of her position and of the possibility of collision to an approaching vessel.

(h/g) A vessel aground shall give the bell signal and if required the gong signal prescribed in paragraph [(g) / (f)] of this Rule and shall, in addition, give three separate and distinct strokes on the bell immediately before and after the rapid ringing of the bell. A vessel aground may in addition sound an appropriate whistle signal.

(i/h) A vessel of less than 12 meters in length shall not be obliged to give the above mentioned signals but, if she does not, shall make some other efficient sound signal at intervals of not more than 2 minutes.

(i) A vessel of 12 meters or more but less than 20 meters in length shall not be obliged to give the bell signals prescribed in paragraphs (g) and (h) of this Rule. However, if she does not, she shall make some other efficient sound signal at intervals of not more than 2 minutes. [Intl]

(j/h) A vessel of less than 12 meters in length shall not be obliged to give the above mentioned signals but, if she does not, shall make some other efficient sound signal at intervals of not more than 2 minutes.

(k/i) A pilotage vessel when engaged on pilotage duty may in addition to the signals prescribed in paragraph (a), (b) or [(g) / (f)] of this Rule sound an identity signal consisting of four short blasts.

(k) The following vessels shall not be required to sound signals as prescribed in paragraph (f) of this Rule when anchored in a special anchorage area designated by the Secretary:

    (i) a vessel of less than 20 meters in length; and

    (i) a barge canal boat, scow, or other nondescript craft. [Inld]

Rule 36 - Signals to Attract Attention

If necessary to attract the attention of another vessel, any vessel may make light or sound signals that cannot be mistaken for any signal authorized elsewhere in these Rules, or may direct the beam of her searchlight in the direction of the danger, in such a way as not to embarrass any vessel. Any light to attract the attention of another vessel shall be such that it cannot be mistaken for any aid to navigation. For the purpose of this Rule the use of high intensity intermittent or revolving lights, such as strobe lights, shall be avoided. [Intl]

Rule 37 - Distress Signals

When a vessel is in distress and requires assistance she shall use or exhibit the signals described in Annex IV to these Regulations.

Rule 37
Distress Signals 72 COLREGS

The distress signals for inland waters are the same as those displayed in the table above with the following additional signal:

Rule 37 - Inland only

A high intensity white light flashing at regular intervals from 50 to 70 times per minute.

PART E - EXEMPTIONS

Rule 38 - Exemptions

International

Any vessel (or class of vessel) provided that she complies with the requirements of the International Regulations for the Preventing of Collisions at Sea, 1960, the keel of which is laid or is at a corresponding stage of construction before the entry into force of these Regulations may be exempted from compliance therewith as follows:

(a) The installation of lights with ranges prescribed in Rule 22, until 4 years after the date of entry into force of these regulations.

(b) The installation of lights with color specifications as prescribed in Section 7 of Annex I to these Regulations, until 4 years after the entry into force of these Regulations.

(c) The repositioning of lights as a result of conversion from Imperial to metric units and rounding off measurement figures, permanent exemption.

(d) (i) The repositioning of masthead lights on vessels of less than 150 meters in length, resulting from the prescriptions of Section 3 (a) of Annex I to these regulations, permanent exemption.

(ii) The repositioning of masthead lights on vessels of 150 meters or more in length, resulting from the prescriptions of Section 3 (a) of Annex I to these regulations, until 9 years after the date of entry into force of these Regulations.

(e) The repositioning of masthead lights resulting from the prescriptions of Section 2(b) of Annex I to these Regulations, until 9 years after the date of entry into force of these Regulations.

(f) The repositioning of sidelights resulting from the prescriptions of Section 2(g) and 3(b) of Annex I to these Regulations, until 9 years after the date of entry into force of these Regulations

(g) The requirements for sound signal appliances prescribed in Annex II to these Regulations, until 9 years after the date of entry into force of these Regulations.

(h) The repositioning of all-round lights resulting from the prescription of Section 9(b) of Annex I to these Regulations, permanent exemption.

Inland

Any vessel or class of vessels, the keel of which is laid or which is at a corresponding stage of construction before December 24, 1980, provided that she complies with the requirements of -
(a) The Act of June 7, 1897 (30 Stat. 96), as amended (33 U.S.C. 154-232) for vessels navigating the waters subject to that statute;
(b) Section 4233 of the Revised Statutes (33 U.S.C. 301-356) for vessels navigating the waters subject to that statute;
(c) The Act of February 8, 1895 (28 Stat. 645), as amended (33 U.S.C. 241-295) for vessels navigating the waters subject to that statute; or
(d) Sections 3, 4, and 5 of the Act of April 25, 1940 (54 Stat. 163), as amended (46 U.S.C. 526 b, c, and d) for motorboats navigating the waters subject to that statute; shall be exempted from compliance with the technical Annexes to these Rules as follows:
(i) The installation of lights with ranges prescribed in Rule 22, until 4 years after the effective date of these Rules, except that vessels of less than 20 meters in length are permanently exempt;

(ii) The installation of lights with color specifications as prescribed in Section 7 of Annex I to these Rules, until 4 years after the effective date of these Rules, except that vessels of less than 20 meters in length are permanently exempt;

(iii) The repositioning of lights as a result of a conversion to metric units and rounding off of measurement figures, are permanently exempt; and.

(iiii) The horizontal repositioning of masthead lights prescribed by Annex I to these Rules:

> (a) on vessels of less than 150 meters in length, permanent exemption.
> (b) on vessels of 150 meters or more in length, until 9 years after the effective date of these Rules.

(iiiii) The restructuring or repositioning of all lights to meet the prescriptions of Annex I to these Rules, until 9 years after the effective date of these Rules;

(iiiiii) Power-driven vessels of 12 meters or more but less than 20 meters in length are permanently exempt from the provisions of Rule 23(a)(i) and 23(a)(iv) provided that, in place of these lights, the vessel exhibits a white light aft visible all round the horizon; and

(iiiiiii) The requirements for sound signal appliances prescribed in Annex III to these Rules, until 9 years after the effective date of these Rules.

Annexes, Interpretative Rules, and other associated Navigation Regulations Not Included in this publication

Annex I - Positioning and Technical Details of Lights and Shapes - International / Inland (33 CFR 84)

Annex II - Additional Signals for Fishing Vessels Fishing in Close Proximity - International / Inland (33 CFR 85)

Annex III - Technical Details of Sound Appliances - International / Inland (33 CFR 86)

Annex IV - Distress Signals - International / Inland (33 CFR 87)

Annex V - Pilot Signals - Inland Only (33 CFR 88)

Interpretive Rules - International (33 CFR 82) / Inland (33 CFR 90)
COLREGS Demarcation Line (33 CFR 80)

Alternate Compliance - International (33 CFR 82) / Inland (33 CFR 90)
Waters Specified by the Secretary - (33 CFR 89.25 - 89.27)
Vessel Bridge-to-Bridge Radiotelephone Regulations - (33 CFR 26)

Vessel Traffic Services (VTS) Call Signs, Designated Frequencies, and Monitoring Areas - 33 CFR Table 161.12(c)

All efforts are made to ensure these Navigation Rules are complete and accurate however the U.S. Coast Guard and the publisher make no claims, promises or guarantees about the accuracy, completeness, or adequacy of the contents and expressly disclaims liability for errors and omissions in the contents.

Those seeking official versions of the Navigation Rules should refer to the International Navigational Rules Act of 1977 (Public Law 95-75, 91 Stat. 308, 33 U.S.C. 1601-1608), and, the Inland Navigation Rules Act of 1980 (Public Law 96-591, 94 Stat. 3415, 33 CFR 83).

USCG NAVIGATION RULES CENTRE.

http://www.navcen.uscg.gov

On this page on the left side one can click for corrections to these rules. .

If you are involved in an accident you should go to this resource and read the FAQ, also Navigation Regulations by Subject.

www.TheBoatBookShop.com